DISTILLERY CATS

DISTILLERY CATS

PROFILES IN COURAGE
OF THE WORLD'S
MOST SPIRITED MOUSERS

BRAD THOMAS PARSONS

ILLUSTRATIONS BY JULIA KUO

TEN SPEED PRESS
California | New York

Copyright © 2017 by Brad Thomas Parsons
Illustrations copyright © 2017 by Julia Kuo

All rights reserved.
Published in the United States by Ten Speed Press,
an imprint of the Crown Publishing Group, a division
of Penguin Random House LLC, New York.
www.crownpublishing.com
www.tenspeed.com

Ten Speed Press and the Ten Speed Press
colophon are registered trademarks of
Penguin Random House LLC.

Library of Congress Cataloging-in-Publication
Data in on file with the publisher.

Hardcover ISBN: 978-1-60774-897-7
eBook ISBN: 978-1-60774-898-4

Printed in China

Design by Lizzie Allen

10 9 8 7 6 5 4 3 2

"YOU KNOW A REAL FRIEND? SOMEONE YOU KNOW WILL LOOK AFTER YOUR CAT AFTER YOU ARE GONE."

—WILLIAM S. BURROUGHS,
LAST WORDS: THE FINAL JOURNALS OF WILLIAM S. BURROUGHS

FOR LOUIS

CONTENTS

INTRODUCTION

For centuries, cats have been punching the clock, helping out humans with odd jobs at the workplace. Granted, "helping" may be too generous a word to use when talking about an animal known to sleep up to twenty hours a day. When they are awake, cats tend to keep to their own schedule and rituals, relying on humans for food, water, and clean litter boxes while doling out warmth and affection at their own whimsy.

When pawing through the Help Wanted ads, cats could find a number of job opportunities they might easily qualify for with little or no experience. There are shop cats who earn their keep curling up in chairs, sprawling on counters, and watching passersby from windows at a wide variety of business establishments, including dry cleaners, real estate offices, florists, and liquor stores. Bookstore cats have a pretty nice life, sleeping among the stacks or curling up in a beam of sunlight in the window display, greeting customers in exchange for a quick scratch or extended petting session. Scrappy bodega cats, the feline denizens of urban corner groceries and convenience stores, have become increasingly well-known in recent years, primarily thanks to social media; their country cousins, pastoral barn cats, have been climbing rafters, mingling with chickens, and napping upon stacks of hay for generations. And then there is the major subcategory of spirited cats, the bar cat, a storied tradition in pubs across the United Kingdom.

While having a charming cat lazing about keeping the shopkeeper company and casually greeting patrons is reason enough to employ one, the historic origin of the feline workforce is primarily in pest control. Dr. Fiona Marshall, a professor of archeology at Washington University in St. Louis, Missouri, wrote a study on the historical domestication of cats and in a 2013 interview with Audie Cornish on NPR's *All Things Considered* notes that while dogs were drawn to humans by the scraps of food they were offered and by the sight of humans hunting, cats, on the other hand, were interested in the by-product of what farmers were growing—the rodents eating the grain.

Enter the distillery cat. (To clarify, I'm using *distillery cat* as an umbrella term that covers brewery cats as well as winery and vineyard cats—the cats that protect our spirits at the source.) For distillers and brewers, wheat, barley, rye, and corn are expensive cash crops, vital to the production of their spirits. For a mouse, rat, or bird, a distillery or brewery may as well be a twenty-four-hour all-you-can-eat buffet. A distillery cat's primary qualifications are to be friendly yet possess the instincts of a cold-blooded killer. In the ongoing battle between cat and mouse, mice are typically pretty quick on the uptake when a distillery cat comes on the scene. After seeing their brothers and sisters go missing in action, mice seek a new venue in which to pester and pilfer to avoid winding up on the hit list.

Historically, Ireland and Scotland have a keen tradition of keeping distillery cats on the payroll and are home to some of the most legendary mousers. A long-haired tortoiseshell dubbed Towser the Mouser lived her twenty-four years at the Glenturret Distillery, Scotland's oldest working distillery, where she ended her career with an estimated kill list of 28,899 mice, giving her the honor of being the *Guinness Book of World Records* "World Mousing Champion." The staff at Dublin's Jameson Distillery was so enamored of their distillery cat, Smitty, that they had him stuffed after his death. He's still on display, positioned atop the rafters of the barley room, posthumously greeting visitors and serving as a deterrent to the local mouse population.

In America, as the boom in craft distilleries and breweries continues to spread across the country, there's a new breed of distillery cats stepping into the spotlight. While these first-generation mousers are delivering on their primal instinct and keeping their homes free of mice, they're also earning their bones in the age of Instagram. These unofficial mascots have become full-fledged brand ambassadors and social-media stars, with many possessing their own dedicated accounts and cat handlers. Their workdays are chronicled online, and taking a selfie with the house distillery cat has become as much a part of the tour experience as free samples of booze. While they still maintain their fiercely independent nature, when they're not sleeping, hunting, or supervising the staff, the modern distillery cat spends a good chunk of the day mingling with patrons in the tasting room.

While the cats are beloved by most, the looming concern over just how sanitary it is to have them on premises at a distillery or brewery does come up. Some cats have been vetted and approved by the local authorities from the county health department, while others have to keep out of the production facility and stay in the front office. I didn't want to rat out any under-the-radar distillery cats, but when I asked distilleries and breweries about this and if there were any particular state laws on the subject, the replies were an equal amount of shrugs, pleading the Fifth, and a repeated refrain of "don't ask, don't tell," although distilleries and breweries that offer food were quick to point out that the cat isn't allowed in the food production area. At most distilleries and breweries, the grain is stored in heavy sacks (which the cat can protect and sleep on, but not eat), and the rest of production—including the grain crusher, kettle, and fermenter—is part of a closed system to maintain a sterile environment.

As an animal lover and longtime cat enthusiast, I will always look the other way in regard to anti-feline ordinances and immediately grab my phone to take a photo when I see a cat hanging out atop a bar or sprawled across a pile of oranges at my local bodega, and the same goes for distilleries. I started the @DistilleryCats Instagram account to chronicle and celebrate the spirited tradition of working cats at distilleries, breweries, wineries, bars, pubs, cafés, and liquor stores. In these pages, you'll read the stories, exploits, and adventures of some of the breakout stars of the new pedigree of American cats embracing their role as guardians of the grain and accidental Internet stars. All cats in the book represent first-generation distillery cats, and nearly all were adopted, rescued from a shelter, abandonment, or life on the streets. The "adopt-don't-shop" ethos supporting animal shelters is strong in this community, and there are amazing groups across the country with a mission to match up members of feral cat colonies with appropriate workplaces like distilleries and breweries as well as warehouses and farms. Hearing about these cats' Dickensian pasts and seeing so many get a second chance at life—and to be loved with abandon—is the most meaningful part of the distillery-cat experience for me. Watching them develop into superstars with their own dedicated fan base is just a perk. Plus, what's not to love about the combination of cats and booze? Let's raise a glass of the good stuff (and pour out a saucer of milk) to distillery cats everywhere.

MEET THE MOUSERS

"I LIKE TO EAT DECORATIVE PLANTS AND TAKE NAPS ON IMPORTANT PAPERS."

7 MONTHS OLD

DOMESTIC SHORTHAIR

FEMALE

CATEGORY BREWERY CAT

FAVORITE SNACK LARGE BUGS

FAVORITE TOY CATNIP-FILLED MOUSE ON A STICK

PRIZED POSSESSION THREE-TIERED SCRATCHING POST

SUPERPOWER ABILITY TO MELT HEARTS OF SO-CALLED PEOPLE WHO DON'T LIKE CATS

AUTOMATIC

AUTO

CREATURE COMFORTS BREWING CO. | ATHENS, GEORGIA

It's only natural that a brewery named Creature Comforts would take in a cat, and like many felines in this line of work, Automatic followed the career trajectory of stray cat turned coworker. As for her name? The little white kitten was discovered trapped in a grain bin at the brewery on the same day they launched their seasonal Automatic Pale Ale into the Athens market, and it seemed a fitting way to commemorate the occasion. She's still too young to have full rein over the entire facility and splits her time between the brewery office and reception area, where this friendly and very energetic cat has embraced her role as brand ambassador. Automatic has already amassed a strong following on social media, where, in addition to chronicling her many naps, she shares regular updates on new releases and events at Creature Comforts (she's particularly fond of Vinyl Wednesdays in the tasting room).

A typical day in the life of this young brewery cat begins when she greets her coworkers as they arrive and then immediately lets everyone know she's ready for her breakfast. The rest of the morning is spent burning off energy by zipping around the office, pinging between her toys, coworkers, and visitors. The remainder of the afternoon is spent catnapping (the potted plant in the reception area is her favorite spot, though shelves, desks, and laptops are fair game) with frequent breaks to welcome brewery visitors coming through for the public tour. Then it's back to the office for dinner and off to sleep.

BLACK HAWK CHINOOK &

SBC SECURITY

SERVICE BREWING CO. | SAVANNAH, GEORGIA

West Point graduate Kevin Ryan, cofounder and CEO of Service Brewing Co., proudly bills his brewery as "veteran owned and veteran brewed," and when he was looking to enlist a cat into service at the brewery he had one mission: "To serve and protect our facility from outsiders that may not be welcome."

Black Hawk and Chinook were just over a month old when they were discovered during construction at the brewery, and both were very ill and suffering from terrible eye infections. After a months-long regimen of six eye drops a day, they were back to health and received their orders to protect 28,000 square feet of territory. The cats are a major attraction on tours and never pass on an opportunity to entertain visitors. Ryan notes that Black Hawk is more of a project manager, "following the brewer around; greeting delivery trucks; observing packaging, keg cleaning, and lunch breaks," while Chinook typically interacts only with larger crowds, always on the lookout for free back scratches.

The tag-team duo spend their days "alternately prowling the uppermost recesses of their territory, keeping encroachers at bay, and batting around keg caps and Ping-Pong balls." They have a keen eye for lizards and deploy military tactics to check for reptilian rivals in empty kegs. "They have not presented us with any perpetrators. We assume they get rid of all the evidence." Another scaly trespasser to put the cats on high alert was a rattlesnake that smuggled itself into the brewery via a shipment of empty beer cans. Ryan notes with pride that "Black Hawk and Chinook were the first to discover the snake, but luckily, we were able to provide reinforcements before they attempted to remove the intruder on their own."

"FIND THE HIGH GROUND. TAKE IT. KEEP IT."

2 YEARS OLD

DOMESTIC SHORTHAIR

MALE

CATEGORY BREWERY CAT

FAVORITE PLACE TO BE SCRATCHED NECK AND SHOULDERS

FAVORITE SNACK ANYTHING THAT TASTES LIKE FISH

FAVORITE TOY KEG CAPS

HOBBY CARDBOARD BOXES

NOTABLE FEATURES BEER BELLY (BLACK HAWK) AND MONKEY TAIL (CHINOOK)

1 YEAR OLD

MAINE COON

MALE

CATEGORY	DISTILLERY CAT
JOB TITLE	OFFICER OF SEX APPEAL
FAVORITE HUMAN BODY PART	ANKLES
FAVORITE TOY	BOTTLE CAPS
SUPERPOWER	TO COLLAPSE HIS BODY AS IF HE WERE BONELESS

BOONE

BOO

THOMAS & SONS DISTILLERY | PORTLAND, OREGON

"We got him off of Craigslist on a whim. Best. Decision. Ever," says Thomas & Sons Distillery Operations Manager Ray Nagler on the origin story of their beloved distillery cat, a Maine coon named Boone. Boone is strictly a nine-to-fiver, commuting to and from the distillery with Nagler, but he's had the travel bug since he was a kitten, when Nagler would carry him around, swaddled in a scarf, to the local farmers' markets, parties, and bars. "He's getting a little too enormous for the scarf. When he was a kitten, I used to take him to an irresponsible amount of dive bars, sometimes covertly." When Boone had too much excitement for the evening, he would go limp and Nagler would drape the sleeping cat over the back of her neck, occasionally passing him around the bar for other patrons to do the same with. "Only one time did we ever get kicked out. It's amazing what bar managers will let you get away with when you've got a kitty in tow."

Nagler recommends other distilleries in the market for a cat look for one that's friendly and "not too spookable," though she's quick to point out that Boone, who is yet to dispatch an unwanted pest, is pretty useless in the security department. "He's lucky he's gorgeous. Have you ever had a friend with no particular skill but was a pleasure to have around? Boone's that guy. Honestly, he's an oaf with zero ability to take care of himself and we love him for it." But in the "people person" department, Boone would get "exceeds expectations" on his annual performance review. His extroverted personality makes him a hit with kids and a sponge for affection. "If he's left in a room without humans, he just waits by the door."

FERNETSCAPE NAVIGATOR

2 OUNCES TOWNSHEND'S
PACIFIC NORTHWEST FERNET

1 OUNCE CYNAR

ORANGE PEEL

Combine all of the ingredients except the orange peel in
a mixing glass filled with ice. Stir until chilled and then
strain into a chilled schnapps glass. Express the orange
peel over the glass rim and discard.

FROM THOMAS & SONS DISTILLERY
PORTLAND, OREGON

MAKES 1 DRINK

"I LIKE TO READ BOOKS.
I LIKE TO LISTEN TO MUSIC.
I COLLECT RECORDS.
AND CATS.
I DON'T HAVE ANY CATS
RIGHT NOW.
BUT IF I'M TAKING A WALK
AND I SEE A CAT,
I'M HAPPY."

—HARUKI MURAKAMI

BREWERY CAT
BUBBLES

Brewery Cat's given name would seem to tell you everything you need to know about her job description at 2SP Brewing Company, but Warehouse and Distribution Manager Joe Ruthig admits that she pretty much runs the show. Brewery Cat's salty online profile is equally succinct: "I'm a cat. I live in a brewery. These are my adventures and sh–t. Boop."

2SP Brewing had just launched a job search for a cat to help with a rodent problem when a dazzlingly cross-eyed stray tabby with a predilection for killing mice came into their lives. When looking over a resume of a prospective distillery cat, Ruthig says there's only one skill to consider: "Kill mice. That's it." The other applicants didn't stand a chance.

Brewery Cat has the run of the facility but is *cattus non grata* at the food prep area, and she's not allowed in the walk-in cooler, which is, of course, the one place she's most interested in exploring. Ruthig describes her as a bit of a loner. "She follows me everywhere, but just hangs out at a distance to just watch me." Like most cats, she loves attention from visitors, but only on her own terms. "You know, typical cat stuff."

Quick reflexes are a must for a working cat, and Brewery Cat is no exception. "She is part spider. I don't know how she gets to some of the spots she gets to. She climbs pallets with ease, and dodges forklifts like it's nothing." Early on, Brewery Cat dispatched three mice ("I think they got the message"), but with the rodent situation locked down she's turned her attention to frogs, moths, and spiders. Flies have proven to be too much of a challenge for her little crossed eyes, though Ruthig assures it's fun to watch her try.

1½ YEARS OLD

TABBY

FEMALE

CATEGORY BREWERY CAT

FAVORITE PLACE TO BE SCRATCHED BEHIND THE EARS
(AND NOWHERE ELSE)

FAVORITE PLACE TO SLEEP POOL TABLE

FAVORITE TOY RUBBER BANDS

HOBBY NAPPING

NOTABLE FEATURE CROSS-EYED

"HUMANS ALWAYS BE WAKING ME UP."

6 YEARS OLD

GINGER

MALE

CATEGORY BREWERY CAT

JOB TITLE GUARDIAN OF THE GRAIN

FAVORITE PLACE TO SLEEP CARDBOARD BOX
BEHIND THE BAR

SNACK ROUTINE TUNA IN THE EVENING

SUPERPOWER SITTING ON LAPS FOR SNUGGLES

BREWSTER
MISTER B

〰

THE GUARDIAN BREWING COMPANY | MUNCIE, INDIANA

The husky, middle-aged, orange creamsicle–colored cat, who would come to be known as Brewster the Brewery Cat, had a dark start in life. Originally, he was known as Max, a scrawny little thing who was a survivor of 110 cats rescued from a hoarder living in a trailer.

Lisa Dunaway, who holds the title of "Cat Coordinator" at the Guardian Brewing Company, was concerned about mice chewing on their expensive grain bags and reached out to a local animal shelter to help her select an appropriate candidate for the newly created position of brewery cat. Enter Max, who was quickly dubbed Brewster. He's come a long way from his Dickensian past; and now he has a beer named after him, the sales of which help benefit the animal shelter where he got a second chance.

When he was first adopted, he was out of shape but quickly developed a routine, shadowing his coworkers and mingling with visitors. Most of the employees build some time into their schedule to play with him during their shift, and the bar's regulars smuggle in treats and catnip toys for him.

Brewster has several beds strategically placed around the brewery for his regular naps, but naturally he prefers a simple cardboard box tucked behind the bar, where he's quickly become a regular, often hopping up to sit on his own barstool that's been dubbed his "throne." "He seems to know that people have come to get a glimpse of him; they get very excited when they see him and will talk to him. The very first day he was here, we announced we had a brew cat, and within two hours, patrons showed up asking to meet him. He adjusted to his new life very quickly."

Much to the disappointment of his many visitors and fans, Brewster's professional career as a brewery cat proved too brief, cut short by an official from the Department of Health. But he's adjusted swimmingly to his civilian life as a home-brew cat.

CASTOR

When two adorable littermates were brought in as kittens, Seattle Distilling held a contest on social media to help name the pair. Top entries included Gin and Tonic, Starsky and Hutch, and, thanks to the familiar-looking little black mustache on one of the kittens, Kitler and Mousolini. The winning names were Castor and Pollux, in honor of the Gemini twins, both legendary hunters.

But as with many partnerships, there were creative differences, and six months into the gig, Pollux hightailed it out of there, moving into the construction offices of Don Roberts, located a block away from the distillery. "Try as we might, we couldn't get him to come home and stay home," says Seattle Distilling CEO Tami Brockway Joyce. But the plot thickened when Pollux, who Roberts renamed Jack, packed up and moved out after a year with Roberts and his family. For six months, a heartbroken Roberts longed for his friend to return home. Then one day on a job site, a familiar little cat sauntered over and hopped up into Roberts' arms.

Unlike his vagabond brother, Castor hasn't had as much drama in his life and quickly acclimated to his role as social butterfly. When he's not fighting for space trying to share Brockway Joyce's office chair, he perches in the rafters of the old log cabin, overseeing the distillation process and keeping an eye out for trouble. Brockway Joyce says, "His presence alone is enough to keep mice away, but once in a while we receive a 'gift,'" adding, "He doesn't tend to leave behind much more than the head."

"IF YOU'RE ALLERGIC TO CATS, DON'T SIT ON MY FAVORITE BARSTOOL."

2½ YEARS OLD

TUXEDO

MALE

CATEGORY DISTILLERY CAT
JOB TITLE STILL UNDER NEGOTIATION
FAVORITE TOY LASER POINTER
NOTABLE FEATURE TOOTHBRUSH MUSTACHE
SUPERPOWER ABILITY TO FIND A WARM LAP

IDLE REVOLVER

1 OUNCE SEATTLE DISTILLING IDLE HOUR WHISKEY

1 OUNCE SEATTLE DISTILLING COFFEE LIQUEUR

1 DASH SCRAPPY'S ORANGE BITTERS

ORANGE PEEL

Combine all of the ingredients except the orange peel
in a mixing glass filled with ice. Stir until chilled
and then strain into a chilled cocktail glass.
Garnish with the orange peel.

FROM SEATTLE DISTILLING | VASHON, WASHINGTON

MAKES 1 DRINK

"WAY DOWN DEEP,
WE'RE ALL MOTIVATED
BY THE SAME URGES.
CATS HAVE THE COURAGE
TO LIVE BY THEM."

—JIM DAVIS

"I EAT WHEN I WANT. I SLEEP WHEN I WANT."

9 YEARS OLD

BLACK AMERICAN SHORTHAIR

FEMALE

CATEGORY DISTILLERY CAT

JOB TITLE KEEPER OF THE BARRELS

FAVORITE TOY I DON'T REALLY PLAY WITH TOYS

HOBBY MINIATURE GOLF

SUPERPOWER GETTING PETTED WHENEVER I WANT

CHAR

Char was a rescue cat, named by the daughter of Oregon Spirit Distillers' owner and adopted to chase away potential vermin at the distillery. The chicken-and-egg scenario to the question, "Does your distillery cat actually catch mice?" goes a little something like this, according to Molly Troupe, production manager and lead distiller: "We haven't seen any evidence of her catching mice. We also haven't seen any evidence of mice. She is hopefully scaring them away with her mere presence."

Char has free run of the barrel house, where her favorite cat bed is set atop a barrel in the corner of the room. Like most cats, Char's typical day involves a lot of sleeping. "She usually comes out in the morning for a brief sunning session before retiring to her barrel bed. In the evening, she'll come out and say hello to people sitting on the patio." Lest you think she wastes her day dreaming away, Char has recently taken up the sport of golf. The barrel house serves double duty as a miniature golf course for distillery visitors, and Char quickly staked her claim to it, stalking the golfers passing through and lying in wait to swipe their balls right out of the hole. "Not only is Char great at her job, she is also the sweetest cat. We feel very lucky to have her."

CHAR'S CHERRY SMASH

4 RIPE CHERRIES, PITTED

5 FRESH MINT LEAVES

1½ OUNCES C. W. IRWIN BOURBON

¾ OUNCE GINGER SYRUP (PAGE 98)

¾ OUNCE FRESH LEMON JUICE

1 DASH ANGOSTURA BITTERS

FRESH MINT SPRIG

Combine the cherries and mint leaves in a cocktail shaker and gently muddle. Add the bourbon, ginger syrup, lemon juice, and bitters, and fill with ice. Shake until chilled and then pour into a double old-fashioned glass filled with ice. Garnish with the mint sprig.

FROM OREGON SPIRIT DISTILLERS | BEND, OREGON

MAKES 1 DRINK

"AND BY THE TIME I'M SOBER
I'VE FORGOTTEN WHAT I'VE HAD
AND EVERYBODY TELLS ME
THAT IT'S COOL TO BE A CAT"

—SQUEEZE, "COOL FOR CATS"

C H O

MR. CHO

SOUND SPIRITS | SEATTLE, WASHINGTON

Cleverly named for the molecular formula of ethanol (C_2H_6O), Cho, was adopted from a local animal shelter by Steven Stone, owner and master distiller at Sound Spirits, the first distillery opened in Seattle since Prohibition. The common refrain for the best qualities of a distillery cat are being a good hunter and getting along with people, and Cho excels on both fronts. "Cho is a very loving cat to everyone lacking fur or feathers, though he does have a healthy aversion to children." In his earlier years, he was an accomplished mouser but has since moved on to what Stone calls "his 'bird' period," adding, "This could be due in part to the fact that we play with him with flying feathers on a string. We might need to revisit his entertainment options."

Cho has outdoor privileges and at night often "cats around" the neighborhood, but in the morning, he's back at the distillery mewing loudly, looking for breakfast (and attention). During the day, he sticks close to his coworkers as the stills are brought up to temperature. "He fancies himself a manager," says Stone. Then it's on to some quick naps atop the grain bags or rolling around in a sunbeam until he settles into his role as "head paperweight" on Stone's desk in the office. But every time he hears the doorbell ding, he runs to greet whomever is in the tasting room. "He doesn't mind if there are two or twenty; he always makes a point to wind his way through everyone to say hello." And Cho definitely has his own fan club. Stone shared that on one day, three different people came into the tasting room, all after the same thing. "They didn't want to buy or sample anything. They just wanted to see 'the amazing black cat' that they had met on the tour."

"EAT. PLAY. NAP."

7 YEARS OLD

BLACK AMERICAN
SHORTHAIR

MALE

CATEGORY DISTILLERY CAT

JOB TITLE HEAD MOUSER

FAVORITE TOY FEATHERS ON A STRING

HOBBY BIRD WATCHING

SUPERPOWER BEING HANDSOME ALL THE TIME

GIN JULEP

1½ OUNCES SOUND SPIRITS OLD TOM GIN

1½ OUNCES EBB + FLOW GIN

½ OUNCE DEMERARA SYRUP (PAGE 98)

12 MINT LEAVES

FRESH MINT SPRIG

Lightly muddle the demerara syrup and mint leaves in a julep cup or double old-fashioned glass. Fill the cup or glass with crushed ice and add the gin. Top with more crushed ice, if needed. Garnish with the mint sprig and serve with a short straw.

FROM SOUND SPIRITS | SEATTLE, WASHINGTON

MAKES 1 DRINK

"I DON'T LIKE LOVE
AS A COMMAND,
AS A SEARCH.
IT MUST COME TO YOU,
LIKE A HUNGRY CAT
AT THE DOOR."

—CHARLES BUKOSWKI, *ON CATS*

"THE DISTILLERY IS MY KINGDOM."

5 YEARS OLD

TABBY

MALE

CATEGORY DISTILLERY CAT

JOB TITLE CHIEF OF SECURITY

FAVORITE PLACE TO BE SCRATCHED EVERYWHERE

FAVORITE TOY A WEIRD STUFFED SEAHORSE

HOBBY KNOCKING UNATTENDED PENS OFF DESKS

SUPERPOWER SLEEPING IN BOXES THAT ARE SLIGHTLY TOO SMALL

COOPER

When United States Senator Chuck Schumer held a press conference at Albany Distilling Co. to launch an initiative to establish crop insurance for local farmers who grow malt barley, this ginger-colored distillery cat stole the show when he hopped up on a barrel next to the podium looking for his own photo op with the senator. Cooper had come a long way from the shape he was in before he was adopted by the distillery. He was turned in to the Troy Veterinary Hospital, woefully malnourished and suffering a deep cut across his torso. They thought he was a goner, but after a month he recovered and now rocks a thirteen-pound frame with a thick coat of fur to cover up his scar. Perhaps never forgetting his rough beginnings, Cooper aggressively demands attention. Albany Distilling Co. President John Curtin notes, "On tours, he will often position himself in front of the crowd. If this isn't enough to garner their attention, he will climb a ladder or stack of barrels to make himself more visible. If this doesn't do it, he will nestle himself inside a visitor's purse."

Curtin compares a distillery cat to a sociopath: "Both are incredibly charming but always ready to kill." Cooper even has his own "mouse dungeon," a defunct drain that's been blocked up with rocks from which there's no escape. "The local wildlife has grown wise to his presence. He used to catch a mouse a day, but now it's rarely even once a month."

In a recent development, Cooper has taken on a protégé at the distillery, a fellow mouser-in-the-making named Montgomery. Here's hoping Montgomery will uphold the tradition of getting into places that require a scissor lift for rescue.

IRONWEED BOULEVARDIER

1½ OUNCES ALBANY DISTILLING CO.
IRONWEED BOURBON WHISKEY

1 OUNCE CAMPARI

1 OUNCE SWEET VERMOUTH

ORANGE TWIST

Combine the bourbon, Campari, and sweet vermouth in
a mixing glass filled with ice. Stir until chilled and then
strain into a double old-fashioned glass over a large ice
cube. Garnish with the orange twist.

FROM ALBANY DISTILLING CO. | ALBANY, NEW YORK
MAKES 1 DRINK

"YOU CAN'T OWN A CAT.
THE BEST YOU CAN DO
IS BE PARTNERS."

—SIR HARRY SWANSON

COPPER

Devoted fans of Corsair's popular distillery cat Pizza (see page 82) have no fear! Copper, the new cat in town, isn't a replacement but has instead taken up residency at another Corsair facility in Nashville.

Copper was found as a street cat. He didn't play nice with the other cats at the adoption facility but was just what Corsair Distillery was looking for. His name was crowd-sourced on Facebook and seemed fitting given his beautiful, shiny coat of fur. Corsair Distillery owner and distiller Darek Bell quickly discovered his new hire's special prowess as an expert mouser before Copper even officially started the job. After the adoption, Bell took Copper to his farmhouse for an adjustment period before punching in at the distillery, but it didn't take the cat long to discover the malt house on the property. "Copper caught a mouse and jumped on the bed where I was working with my laptop and released it right next to me. I nearly leaped out of bed in shock."

Copper's main role at the distillery is pest control, but he's a natural at tourism and hospitality. "He loves visitors and enjoys being a part of the tours, except when he gets in a pissy mood. He is very affectionate when not being a complete brat. Basically, he has the standard cat operating system." Copper also has a knack for being an in-house morale booster for the team. "Bottling is a tough job, as it is so repetitive and monotonous. Copper loves to come out on bottle day, and I think he does it to lift people's spirits, even though they are sweating buckets and he is just sitting there lazing about."

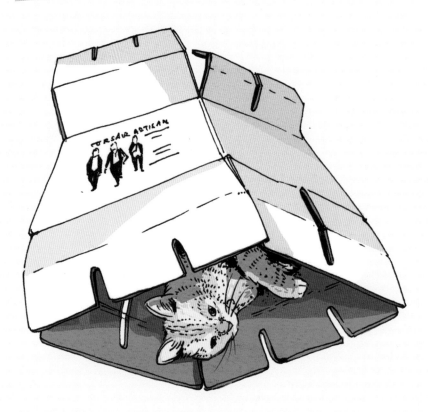

"I ENJOY HANGING WITH PEOPLE, BUT I ENJOY SLEEPING EVEN MORE."

7 MONTHS OLD

AMERICAN SHORTHAIR

MALE

CATEGORY DISTILLERY CAT

JOB TITLE HEAD MOUSER

FAVORITE POSSESSION CAT BED MADE OUT OF A BARREL

FAVORITE TOY *STAR WARS* BB-8 PLUSH TOY

SUPERPOWER RODENT ANNIHILATION

FALL FASHIONED

1½ OUNCES CORSAIR OATRAGE WHISKEY
¼ OUNCE COLD-BREWED COFFEE
¼ OUNCE DEMERARA SYRUP (PAGE 98)
ORANGE PEEL

Combine all of the ingredients except the orange peel in a mixing glass filled with ice. Stir until chilled and then strain into a chilled old-fashioned glass filled with ice. Garnish with the orange peel.

FROM CORSAIR DISTILLERY | NASHVILLE, TENNESSEE
MAKES 1 DRINK

"HOW YOU BEHAVE
TOWARD CATS
HERE BELOW
DETERMINES YOUR STATUS
IN HEAVEN."

—ROBERT A. HEINLEIN

"I'M THE PERFECT BALANCE BETWEEN A STEALTHY ASSASSIN AND A GENTLE, LOVING, FURRY FRIEND."

1 YEAR OLD

TORTOISESHELL

FEMALE

CATEGORY DISTILLERY CAT

JOB TITLE SHIPPING BOX SPECIALIST

BEST FRIEND FLO THE DISTILLERY DOG

FAVORITE TOY FEATHER WITH BELLS

SUPERPOWER CAMOUFLAGE

CORK

CORKY PANTS

OLDE YORK FARM DISTILLERY AND COOPERAGE |
HUDSON, NEW YORK

Since Olde York Farm is located in a barn on a property with a working farmhouse, the distillery cat, Cork, also has the unique skillset of her country cousin, the barn cat. Cork was feral before she was adopted from a nearby shelter.

Olde York Farm's owner and operator Sophie Newsome recalls that when they went to adopt, Cork, unlike the other kittens in the pen who were sleeping, was running around bopping her cellmates on the head causing a ruckus. "The first thing Rory, our head distiller, said was, 'She's the one. This one's a killer.' There was something about the spunky look in her eyes and her athletic stature that you could just tell."

Newsome adds, "We love cats for their companionship and quirky, playful personalities. But on a working farm, a distillery cat also has the important job of pest control." Cork, named for the texture and colors of her brindle coat, has that covered, catching mice at least three times a week, and always leaving her "presents" by the side door of the house to be discovered by her humans the next day.

During the day, Cork hangs out in the cooperage, where she oversees the team's barrel-making duties, jumping from barrel to barrel until she finds the perfect one to nap on. Every day, Cork chases Flo the distillery dog in circles until they're both exhausted, but it's the distillery ducks—Gin, Juniper, Malt, Mash, and Heart—who have a bit of a crush on Cork. "For some reason, the ducks are obsessed with Cork and follow her 'round our backyard. Cork is extremely skeptical about this."

CELERY TONIC

12 CELERY LEAVES

¼ OUNCE FRESH LIME JUICE

1½ OUNCES DIAMOND STREET VODKA

½ OUNCE BUDDHA'S HAND
MICRO BATCH VODKA

5 DASHES FEE BROTHERS RHUBARB BITTERS

4 DASHES CELERY BITTERS

PREMIUM TONIC WATER

1 SHORT CELERY STALK

Lightly muddle the celery leaves and lime juice in the bottom of a mixing glass. Add both vodkas, rhubarb bitters, and celery bitters and stir until chilled. Strain into a double old-fashioned glass filled with ice and top with tonic water. Garnish with the celery stalk.

FROM OLDE YORK FARM | HUDSON, NEW YORK

MAKES 1 DRINK

"WHEN A MAN
LOVES CATS,
I AM HIS FRIEND
AND COMRADE,
WITHOUT FURTHER
INTRODUCTION."

—MARK TWAIN

DARYL HALL

LUCKY HARE BREWING COMPANY | HECTOR, NEW YORK

Ian Conboy, vice president and head brewer at Lucky Hare Brewing Company, cut a deal with a local architecture firm. "If I brought beer up to their drinking club and gave a little presentation about the brewery, one of the architects would exchange two barn cats for my time. It was a hell of a deal." As a longtime fan of the sweet Philly soul sounds of Hall and Oates, Conboy naturally dubbed the two feline brothers Daryl Hall and John Oates. Sadly, John Oates is no longer with us (RIP), but his brother Daryl has lived up to his potential and honors John Oates's memory each and every day on the job. "Hopefully this guy stays around for a long time because he has a great demeanor and is a terror to all mice in the brewery." For now, Daryl is a strictly catch-and-release mouser, but he did once claim an unfortunate barn swallow for his trophy case.

Daryl resides in the brewery most of the week. "He pretty much runs around like a lunatic searching for bugs and mice. Daryl then naps for most of the day behind the buckets where I keep all of my sanitary fittings." But on weekends, it's all about mixing and mingling with visitors in the busy taproom. His primary role may be pest patrol, but he's pretty good at keeping patrons around to order another beer.

"We were hoping to have a cat who would hunt for parts of the day but also be chill in the brewery. Daryl has exceeded those expectations and has become a super-friendly bar cat too. Plus, the ladies fall in love with him at first sight."

"BECAUSE YOUR KISS IS ON MY LIST."

4 MONTHS OLD

TABBY

MALE

CATEGORY BREWERY CAT

JOB TITLE TAPROOM HAM

FAVORITE TOY ANYTHING SHINY

I'M REALLY INTO . . . DOGS

SUPERPOWER CAN STAND UP LIKE A PRAIRIE DOG

THE DUCLAWS

DUCLAW BREWING CO. | BALTIMORE, MARYLAND

MOSAIC

HELLRAZER

"TAKING NAMES AND MELTING HEARTS."

BOCK

SIMCOE

8 MONTHS OLD

TABBY

MALE & FEMALE

CATEGORY BREWERY CATS
JOB TITLE AMERICA'S SWEETHEARTS
FAVORITE TOY EACH OTHER
HOBBY MODELING
SUPERPOWER TRICKS FOR TREATS

When DuClaw Brewing Co. moved into their new facility, Vice President of Operations Elizabeth Hanfman joked that they should get a brewery cat to keep the mice away. When she heard that a litter of stray kittens was living under the back deck of one their employees, she decided to adopt two of them. But once she saw that lineup, she couldn't pick just two. Each of the brew crew's adopted names are related to beer in some way. HellRazer is named after one of the brewery's signature beers, Simcoe and Mosaic are varieties of hops, and Bock, a style of beer. "When we rescued the cats, they had not been around people or inside before. The kittens were terrified, and HellRazer would attack anyone who came near her or the other kittens. Thankfully, she warmed up to us after a while."

Since their big reveal on social media, the quartet informally known as HellRazer and the DuClaws have generated mop-top-era Beatlemania-like enthusiasm among cat lovers and beer drinkers alike. The laidback cats even have their own John, Paul, George, and Ringo shorthand descriptors: the boss (HellRazer), the lion (Simcoe), the princess (Mosaic), and the runt (Bock).

HellRazer loves to interact but is pretty selective about who she gets cuddly with at the office. People fall in love when they take one look at Simcoe's face, but "of course the cat who draws the most attention is the cat that doesn't really care for it. He prefers to be with the group and isn't into being held. He'll allow you the privilege for about five minutes, but then he is off getting into trouble." On the other hand, Mosaic and her brother Bock can't get enough attention and are both busy participating in a daily training routine to learn tricks. "Bock especially is easily trainable mostly because he is food oriented." Mosaic also sits in on the weekly marketing meeting. "When she is not laying in someone's lap, she is sitting on a conference chair watching the presentation on the TV, just fascinated.

"They should be hunting, but they mostly just play. They have brought in a dead bird and on several occasions have brought me [a] mousetrap with the dead mouse in them. So there is hope."

"WE'RE SO
WONDERFULLY
WONDERFULLY
WONDERFULLY
WONDERFULLY
PRETTY!"

—THE CURE, "LOVE CATS"

"ANYTHING THE LIGHT TOUCHES IS MY KINGDOM."

HOTEL TANGO WHISKEY:
DSP-IN-21004:
PRODUCT:
DATE FILLED:
ALC. BY VOL:

2 YEARS OLD

PIXIE BOB

MALE

CATEGORY DISTILLERY CAT

JOB TITLE MOUSER IN CHIEF

FAVORITE TOY OFFICE PRINTER

HOBBY RECREATIONAL CATNIP

I'LL NEVER SAY NO TO . . . A GOOD RUBDOWN

FLETCHER PICKLES

FLETCH

HOTEL TANGO ARTISAN DISTILLERY | INDIANAPOLIS, INDIANA

While there's a lot of "don't ask, don't tell" when it comes to the legalities of having a distillery cat on premises, Fletcher Pickles is free and clear as he's registered as an Emotional Service Animal for Travis Barnes, one of the distillery's owners who is a combat-disabled veteran. Barnes was doing research on distillery traditions, and the historic role of cats and distilleries was one of his favorite topics. After the research, he and co-owner Brian Willsey picked up an eight-week-old kitten. Willsey admits, "We paid a lot of money for Fletcher, much to the chagrin of our investors. However, because he is used as a piece of equipment to keep the grains safe from mice, Fletcher is a tax write-off. He paid for himself pretty quickly, based on the number of calls we get a week asking if he is on duty before a party comes to the distillery."

Named after Indianapolis's historic Fletcher Place neighborhood, home of the distillery, Fletcher lives at the distillery with occasional sleep-away-camp visits to Willsey's home. Early on, he hunted down fifteen mice, but after the first few months, the mice knew they had met their match and left for good. One of his most famous incidents came about after "he got all messed up on some really powerful Colombian-grade catnip" and got twisted in a nest of flypaper strips. Panicked, he ran to his litter box and rolled around, covering himself with kitty litter. For the next month, following a trip to the vet, who had to cut off the clumps of kitty-litter-covered hair, Fletcher resembled a cat who had "escaped a near-death experience with a wood chipper."

He quickly developed a devoted fan base and stepped into his role as the Hotel Tango mascot, with nearly as many Instagram followers as the actual distillery. "I suspect he sees himself as the Brad Pitt of cats. Women love him, knowing that he will eventually hurt them. However, they can't help themselves because he is so goddamn handsome."

BATTLE OF OL' CHARLIE

2 OUNCES LIMA CHARLIE LIMONCELLO

½ OUNCE FRESH LEMON JUICE

½ OUNCE SIMPLE SYRUP (PAGE 99)

2 DASHES ANGOSTURA BITTERS

LEMON PEEL

Combine all of the ingredients except the lemon peel in a mixing glass filled with ice. Stir until chilled and then strain into a double old-fashioned glass over a large ice cube. Garnish with the lemon peel.

FROM HOTEL TANGO ARTISAN DISTILLERY | INDIANAPOLIS, INDIANA

MAKES 1 DRINK

"BOOKS. CATS.
LIFE IS GOOD."

—EDWARD GOREY

"GANGSTA CAT DOESN'T PLAY NICE."

4 TO 5 YEARS OLD

GRAY AND WHITE

FEMALE

CATEGORY BREWERY CAT

FAVORITE HUMAN BODY PART LAP (BUT ONLY ON HER TERMS)

FAVORITE TOY GANGSTA CAT DOESN'T HAVE TIME FOR TOYS

HOBBY PUTTING THE SQUEEZE ON WEAKER CATS

NUMBER OF MICE APPREHENDED UNKNOWN

GANGSTA CAT

THE MAYOR

OTHER HALF BREWING CO. | BROOKLYN, NEW YORK

Usually it's the business that seeks out a distillery cat, but sometimes the cat finds you. The feline that would become known as Gangsta Cat was already living in a colony next to Brooklyn's Other Half Brewing Co. in the industrial neighborhood of Gowanus. When they first opened, Director of Sales Joe Harer remembers her stopping by to check out the new tenants, and while Gangsta Cat still calls the cat colony home, in the winter months she takes up residence at the brewery. She got her badass street name after harassing Other Half owner and master brewer Sam Richardson's dog.

Gangsta Cat still makes her rounds, exploring the alleys that connect the backyards of the apartments next door, but comes back to "strut down her turf and pop in for a snack." Beyond intimidating the other neighborhood strays, she likes the attention of visitors but always on her own terms. "She likes to post up right in the center of the party and won't turn down a good pat, but if you cross her line, you'll know it. She didn't get that name for nothing. She's known to show up when the taproom starts hopping, and to leave when the crowds go away. Gangsta Cat doesn't like weak parties."

Harer thinks of Gangsta as more of a neighbor or regular who sometimes crashes on your sofa rather than a full-fledged feline ambassador for Other Half Brewing Co. "She marches to her own beat. Legend has it that someone once tried to take her home and adopt her. She messed up the inside of their house badly enough that they wisely returned her to her home on Centre Street." And does Gangsta actually catch any mice? "We've never seen one inside of our space after three years, so we're pretty sure she's doing something right."

GENERAL PATTON

GENERAL PEEPEE

NEVERSINK SPIRITS | PORT CHESTER, NEW YORK

The team at Neversink Spirits once borrowed a cat from a colleague to live in the distillery for a few weeks as a test run. Manager Yoni Rabino says, "He was a sweet cat but shy and reserved. He didn't really have the temperament to be a distillery cat." Enter General Patton, a former stray who came from the shelter with his commanding given name already in place due to his bossy nature. "Patton, on the other hand, is confident and independent. He walks around like he owns the place, which is exactly what we were looking for."

The "talkative" General keeps a regular, disciplined routine. In the morning, he follows his coworkers around as they set up the still and ready the production line. By late morning, he's retired to his favorite spot in the ceiling above the bathroom, where he camps out for a few hours. He'll stop by around lunch, especially if what everyone's eating smells good, before going back to his bathroom perch or climbing to the top of his "box throne" (a cardboard box atop a giant pile of other cardboard boxes).

"He loves people more than any other cat we've met. He will always want to approach visitors, talk (meow), and ideally jump in their laps. If the visitor is walking around, he'll follow close behind." Patton is occasionally let outside to roam for a while when the weather is nice, but one day he went on a secret mission and didn't return per usual. Rabino left food and water outside, hoping for Patton's reappearance. The next morning, they got a call from a business nearby. Patton had clandestinely slipped into a neighboring furniture warehouse and had set up base camp among the comfortable chairs and sofas inside. "He was returned safely, acted like nothing happened, and immediately went back to his usual routine.

"IF A GLIMMER OF A LAP APPEARS, I'M ON IT IN A FLASH."

2 YEARS OLD

TABBY

MALE

CATEGORY DISTILLERY CAT

JOB TITLE THE BOSS

FAVORITE TOY CORKS

SKILLS MICROSOFT OFFICE

SUPERPOWER ABILITY TO FIND WARM LAPS

PATTON PARFAIT

HERBETET GÉNÉPY DES ALPES OR ABSINTHE FOR RINSE

1½ OUNCES NEVERSINK UNAGED APPLE BRANDY

¾ OUNCE FRESH LEMON JUICE

½ OUNCE FRAMBOISE LIQUEUR

½ OUNCE SIMPLE SYRUP (PAGE 99)

1 EGG WHITE

3 DASHES ANGOSTURA BITTERS

1 APPLE SLICE

1 FRESH RASPBERRY

Rinse a chilled cocktail glass with Herbetet Génépy des Alpes. Combine the brandy, lemon juice, framboise liqueur, simple syrup, and egg white in a cocktail shaker and dry shake (without ice) for at least 15 seconds. Add ice to the shaker and shake until chilled. Strain into the chilled, rinsed coupe glass and carefully float the bitters on the surface. Garnish with the apple slice and raspberry on a pick.

FROM NEVERSINK SPIRITS | PORT CHESTER, NEW YORK

CREATED BY JUSTIN LANE BRIGGS

MAKES 1 DRINK

"STRAY CAT STRUT

I'M A LADIES' CAT

I'M A FELINE CASANOVA

HEY MAN THAT'S THAT"

—STRAY CATS, "STRAY CAT STRUT"

"OUR BARRELS HAVE NEVER BEEN IN SAFER MITTENS."

9 MONTHS OLD

DOMESTIC SHORTHAIR

MALE

CATEGORY DISTILLERY CAT

JOB TITLE MOUSER

FAVORITE TOY FLIES

NOTABLE FEATURE EXTRA TOES

SUPERPOWER SNEAKING THROUGH DOORS JUST AS THEY'RE ABOUT TO CLOSE

HEMINGWAY & HANCOCK

LEBOWSKI & THUMBS

MIDDLE WEST SPIRITS | COLUMBUS, OHIO

The two tabbies Hancock (slate gray) and Hemingway (orange and white) are a pair of polydactyl cats, that is, born with extra digits on their front paws. More casually known as "Hemingway cats," their adopted names derive from Ernest Hemingway, who was enamored of polydactyl cats and kept many of them at his Key West estate where generations of offspring still roam the grounds. Hancock (the middle name of one of Hemingway's sons) is more frequently called Thumbs, as his extra digits are nearly as big as his whole paw. But according to Middle West Spirits Operations Manager Kelly Locker, it remains uncertain whether these extra claws come in handy on rodent patrol duties. "We found them playing with a couple of dead mice once, but it's uncertain if they actually killed them."

Hemmingway, also known as "Lebowski" due to his chilled-out attitude, is all about the human interaction, while Hancock tends to be a little standoffish. "He likes attention, but usually only in small doses," says Locker. It's not uncommon to go all day without seeing him; he finds a place to hide and naps there. But Hemingway is always prowling for affection from employees and visitors. "He is super-lovable and loves to snuggle and be held and [to get] lots of kisses." Not too long after they got the cats, Hemingway was accidentally left outside for the night. The next morning, they found him crying in the bushes, with cuts on his face and several missing back claws. He was fine after a full day of sleeping on the job, but the team jokes that this was his "initiation." "He was a getting a little soft, so we think this toughened him up a bit."

SHORT NORTH PAWSEE

1½ OUNCES MIDDLE WEST SPIRITS
VIM & PETAL GIN

1 OUNCE CAMPARI

1 OUNCE FRESH ORANGE JUICE

1 OUNCE SODA WATER

ORANGE PEEL

Combine all of the ingredients except the orange
peel in a Collins glass filled with ice and stir.
Garnish with the orange peel.

FROM MIDDLE WEST SPIRITS | COLUMBUS, OHIO

MAKES 1 DRINK

"A CAT HAS ABSOLUTE EMOTIONAL HONESTY; HUMAN BEINGS, FOR ONE REASON OR ANOTHER, MAY HIDE THEIR FEELINGS, BUT A CAT DOES NOT."

—ERNEST HEMINGWAY

HOODIE

NEWBURGH BREWING COMPANY | NEWBURGH, NEW YORK

In the annals of street cats turned brewery cats, Newburgh Brewing Company's Hoodie looms large. As the story goes, she started off in Brooklyn, "fending off the most ardent of hipsters while roaming the streets of Williamsburg" until her life took a turn for the better after meeting a certain brewmaster. When Christopher Basso started his car on a cold Brooklyn morning, he heard a distinctive series of meows over the noise of the engine. His search for a cat came up empty, so he drove to work. After his shift, he heard the same series of meows coming from his car, but this time he popped the hood and out popped Hoodie, who had been hiding within the engine block of the car to stay warm. She ran off into a nearby parking lot, but Basso gave chase and was able to scoop up the hitchhiking cat.

Hoodie got her first taste of the working life when she interned for a few weeks at Brooklyn Brewery—where Basso was a brewer—under the tutelage of Monster (RIP), one of Kings County's most legendary mousers. A kind woman named Jessica Mullin (now married to Newburgh Brewing Company's president and co-owner Paul Halayko) took Hoodie in until their new brewery opened in Newburgh, New York, where Hoodie has since become the unofficial mascot. Visitors to the brewery are constantly asking to take a selfie with the noted feline, and she is always happy to oblige.

During business hours, Hoodie sticks close to Halayko, typically sprawling out over the paperwork on his desk. But at night she goes on rodent patrol. The running tally of KIA mice is fifty-seven over four years (that they know of), and she typically leaves the remains in Halayko's office or the office bathroom.

"DRAW ME LIKE ONE OF YOUR FRENCH CATS."

6 YEARS OLD

TABBY

FEMALE

CATEGORY BREWERY CAT

JOB TITLE CONTROLLER AND GENERAL ACCOUNTING MANAGER

FAVORITE TOY FAKE STUFFED BIRD ON A STRING

HOBBY SCRATCHING EXPENSIVE THINGS

NUMBER OF MICE APPREHENDED 57

"MEOW, BABY!"

1 YEAR OLD

TUXEDO

FEMALE

CATEGORY BREWERY CAT
JOB TITLE OPERATIONS SUPERVISOR
FAVORITE TOY FRISBEE
PEOPLE SAY I'M A . . . MICROMANAGER
SUPERPOWER CLIMBING LADDERS

HOPS

Hops the brew cat lives up to her name at her day job and with her high level of energy, bouncing around entertaining coworkers and patrons alike. She's an expert at playing hide-and-seek and has a weakness for cardboard-box forts. Zaftig Brewing Co. owner Jim Gokenbach suspects the former farm cat from Indiana may be part collie, judging from her prowess chasing after Frisbees. Though she has no confirmed kills just yet, she works the nightshift keeping the building free of intruders. But during the day, she embraces her role as queen of the brewery. In the morning, she follows the staff around, watching over daily operations from her favorite perch high up in the rafters. She'll then sun herself atop pallets of grain bags lined up under a row of windows before settling into her "safe place," a plush cat bed that rests a wooden barrel. She then washes up and at four o'clock hits the taproom to mingle with guests. "She loves interacting with customers, especially children."

JAMES

JIMBO

RUSHING DUCK BREWING CO. | CHESTER, NEW YORK

Rushing Duck Brewing Co. co-owner Nikki Cavanaugh adopted James as a kitten, but when apartment-lease issues forbidding a cat arose, Cavanaugh drafted him into service at the brewery she was opening. "He's like a family member to us, and we didn't want to give him up so we decided to see if he would enjoy brewery life. He adapted to it quickly, and now this is his kingdom." James has a favorite nest above the tasting room where he retires for privacy and long naps, but he has full access to the facility and even patrols the outside perimeter of the building, keeping the parking lot cricket-free.

James isn't wild about other cats and holds his own against dogs, "but he's rocking a major crush on the UPS deliverywoman, who brings him treats along with the daily packages." When the tasting room is open, James posts up in a cardboard box atop a barstool next to customers and demands that they pet him or give him head scratches.

After the sun goes down and the business closes for the day, he's on the hunt in the grain room. One of James's most epic battles was with a large rat that lived in the foundation of the building. "James became obsessed with hunting him," and for two weeks he would walk into the brewery and sit by the door looking for the rat, who was known as Raul. "One day we were looking at James's face, noticed he had a few small cuts, and realized he got into a fight with something. A few minutes later we found Raul dead in the corner. James was so proud of his kill that he wanted to share his trophy with his beloved coworkers." James was declared a hero of Rushing Duck.

"A WILLINGNESS TO HUNT IS THE BEST WORKING QUALITY."

7 YEARS OLD

TABBY

MALE

CATEGORY BREWERY CAT
JOB TITLE HEAD MOUSER
ARCHENEMY RAUL THE RAT
FAVORITE TOY CARDBOARD BOX WITH CATNIP INSIDE
SECRET ADMIRER UPS DELIVERYWOMAN

"NO SLEEP 'TILL BROOKLYN."

4 TO 5 YEARS OLD

DOMESTIC
SHORTHAIR

MALE

CATEGORY DISTILLERY CAT

JOB TITLE RODENT-ERADICATOR EMERITUS

BEST FRIEND CARLOS

FAVORITE TOY BALL OF USED BLUE MASKING TAPE

SUPERPOWER CAN KNOCK ON DOORS

JEFFY

Jeffy began his esteemed career as one half of Brooklyn's most buzzed-about distillery cat duos, Carlos and Jeffy. Colin Spoelman, master distiller and cofounder of Kings County Distillery (the first new operating distillery in New York City since Prohibition), fondly remembers the late Carlos, a gregarious tuxedo cat who succumbed to an urban feline illness. "He was very bloodthirsty, which was of great use to us in the distillery, so we were especially sad to see him go. Jeffy is pretty much retired now, though he does chase birds off the loading dock and around the spent grain bins."

Jeffy still lives in the distillery, "sitting on grain totes, skulking along the wall behind the fermenters, sleeping, stalking the birds in the corn garden, greeting visitors," but is allowed to roam the grounds and abandoned buildings in the historic Brooklyn Navy Yard. The distillery had been pest-free for nearly a year until Hurricane Sandy flooded the building and the surrounding area, washing in waves of "roving bands of displaced zombie mice." The damaged bags of grain spilled over the flooded distillery floor made them an easy target for hungry, nomadic mice on the hunt for a meal. After three weeks on the job, Carlos and Jeffy helped with cleanup, and, Spoelman reports, "the problem was solved."

Spoelman respects the privacy of the introverted Jeffy, who spends most of his free time in his little cat bed atop a giant sack of corn in a room that had previously been both a lab and the employee break room before being transformed into the "Cat Lab." "Jeffy is an employee, so what he does in his private life is his own business. We don't ask so long as the job he was hired to do is getting done—and so far he's earning his keep."

WATERMELON PUNCH

½ OUNCE SIMPLE SYRUP (PAGE 99)

6 FRESH BASIL LEAVES

½ OUNCE FRESH LEMON JUICE

1½ OUNCES KINGS COUNTY DISTILLERY
MOONSHINE

FRESHLY SQUEEZED WATERMELON JUICE

Lightly muddle the simple syrup and basil leaves in a
double old-fashioned glass. Fill with ice, add the lemon
juice and moonshine, and top with watermelon juice.

FROM KINGS COUNTY DISTILLERY
BROOKLYN, NEW YORK
MAKES 1 DRINK

"CATS WERE THE GANGSTERS OF THE ANIMAL WORLD, LIVING OUTSIDE THE LAW AND OFTEN DYING THERE. THERE WERE A GREAT MANY OF THEM WHO NEVER GREW OLD BY THE FIRE."

—STEPHEN KING, *PET SEMATARY*

LELAND MURPHY

ROCKAWAY BREWING COMPANY | LONG ISLAND CITY, NEW YORK

It's always heartbreaking when you go to check in on a favorite brewery or distillery cat only to learn that they're no longer with us. Among those felines fallen on the job was a gray-and-brown tabby named Leland Murphy, who, in 2016, succumbed to his lifelong battle with feline leukemia. The coworkers and friends he left behind at the Rockaway Brewing Company have ensured that his memory will live on.

Leland Murphy (who always went by his full name) started out as a street cat from Williamsburg, Brooklyn. Brewer Flint Whistler recalls that the brewmaster's young daughter chose the name Leland Murphy, but when pressed for the reasoning behind it she refused to clarify. "He was a stray cat that started showing up in our brewmaster's backyard asking for food and affection. He was incredibly friendly and affectionate, so they wanted to adopt him. Since he had feline leukemia, he was unable to live with their other cats, so the brewery could provide him with a nice, comfortable home."

After he passed, Leland Murphy was cremated and given a proper wake, complete with a bagpiper, and Whistler lovingly recalls the brew house being packed with people who came to pay their respects. After a touching eulogy from the brewmaster, Whistler finished the proceeding with a whiskey toast, and the rest of the evening was spent telling stories of Leland Murphy's incredibly affectionate nature and his renowned fearlessness when battling dogs (Leland Murphy always seemed to forget they ran a dog-friendly brewery). "He never lost a confrontation with a dog, and never failed to nuzzle a new person or spend time with a child." RIP, Leland Murphy.

"HE WAS JUST SO INCREDIBLY FRIENDLY."

RIP

TABBY

MALE

CATEGORY BREWERY CAT

LELAND MURPHY IS MISSED BY ALL WHO KNEW HIM.

2 YEARS OLD

TABBY

MALE & FEMALE

CATEGORY DISTILLERY CAT

JOB TITLE DISTILLERY CAT

BEST FRIEND NINA THE AUSTRALIAN SHEPHERD

FAVORITE TOY BARREL BUNGS

SUPERPOWER TIPPING OVER WASTEBASKETS

MASHER & TWO-ROW

Adopted as kittens to help "prevent the mouse population from getting a foothold" at Hamilton Distillers, the brother-and-sister team of Masher and Two-Row have delivered on their reputation. Distiller Stephen Paul calls Masher "a rough and tumble guy" and "sweet as all get-out, but a boy all the way." What was the origin of their quirky names? "Since we mash barley every day, Masher seemed a good moniker. We mash with two-row barley, so Two-Row was the natural name for his sister. She's definitely prettier than he is."

Masher, a born entertainer, specializes in hijacking public distillery tours with his antics. "He's the more aggressively friendly one, and so gets *a lot* of attention from cat lovers." His sister, who despite her standoffishness is equally popular with distillery visitors, keeps her distance from everyone except Paul. When the opportunity presents itself, she's quick to hop on his lap and knead his stomach with her paws. "We've never actually seen either of them with a mouse. I guess they have a lot of down time."

In their two years together, both cats have already dipped into one of their respective nine lives. During a treacherous climb atop a stack of shipping pallets filled with bottles, Two-Row launched herself to the top of an eighteen-foot-high malt-storage silo. Unable to gain purchase on the slick, angled steel top of the silo, she crashed to the floor with a thud. As for Masher, while seeking out a warm spot to curl up under the boiler, he accidentally singed his fur and darted across the distillery floor, leaving a trail of smoke in his wake.

OLD HORATIO
KITTY

SEVENTH SON BREWING CO. | COLUMBUS, OHIO

Seventh Son Brewing Co.'s Colin Vent had given a brewery cat a try, but it just didn't work out. "We had one other cat for a few weeks, but he was very meek and spent most of his time hiding—even though he weighed more than twenty-five pounds. He ended up going home with one of the owners' kids." But when Vent's wife encountered a stray, skinny little kitten on the sidewalk on her way to work, he decided to give it another shot. Old Horatio has been there ever since. While he also travels under the more official-sounding title of assistant bar manager, his proper name floated to the top of the short list of names due to the brewery's bartenders mishearing their house beer, Golden Ratio, as "Old Horatio."

Old Horatio is well-behaved and sleeps far too much, in Vent's opinion, but "once the bar opens, he generally strolls around letting girls pick him up to cuddle."

He likes to "poke around the malt bags" looking for something to kill, and living in an old building, he sees his seasonal share of mouse activity. "He generally nails one or two in a short period of time, then the rest stay away." Along with all the mice, several birds have fallen victim to his claws, and "he once found two baby bunnies, but they were safely extracted and released." But even when Old Horatio is hanging around the bar minding his own business, he seems to cause a stir. "His collar has my phone number on it, so I routinely get late-night texts and phone calls from drunk folks worried that he's lost. I always tell them to set him down, he lives at the brewery, and thank you for your concern."

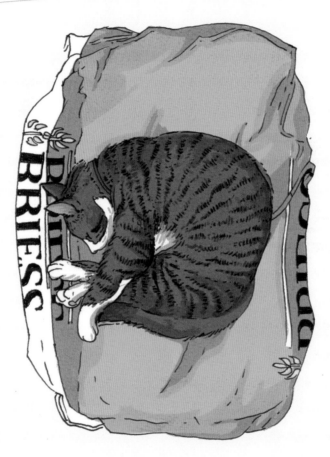

3 YEARS OLD

TABBY

MALE

CATEGORY BREWERY CAT

JOB TITLE ASSISTANT MANAGER

FAVORITE TOY PEOPLE'S LEGS

NUMBER OF MICE APPREHENDED 20

SUPERPOWER LADIES' MAN

"SLEEP. EAT. FROLIC. REPEAT."

2 YEARS OLD

TABBY

MALE

CATEGORY	DISTILLERY CAT
I'M REALLY INTO . . .	FROLICKING
DON'T EVEN THINK ABOUT . . .	RUBBING HIS BELLY
FAVORITE TOY	MICE
SUPERPOWER	DOES WHATEVER THE HELL HE WANTS

PEPPER

When a mother cat abandoned her litter of kittens just before a November freeze, Orange County Distillery co-owner Bryan Ensall came to the rescue. Two of the cats went home to live with Ensall, while their brother, Pepper, took on the responsibility of distillery cat. But an indentured servant he is not. "He doesn't work unless it pleases him. Pepper's lived at the distillery his whole life, so he's adapted to a life that suits him only." It's a life best summed up as "sleeping and frolicking," but he makes time for chasing birds and dismembering mice on a daily basis.

When visitors stop by the distillery and ask, "Where's Pepper?" the answer is almost always, "He's sleeping." He eats in one place, but sleeps wherever he likes, usually interfering with production in the process, curling up in plastic buckets or in repose on a pile of corks. He seems immune to noise and tends to sleep in the loudest parts of the distillery.

Ensall and his team have quickly gotten used to Pepper's independent spirit. "If it's cold out, we will try to get him inside for the night. If we don't, he knows to go to a neighbor's house and yell at the front door until it opens. If it's warm out, he does what he wants."

A BARN CAT NAMED PEPPER

2 OUNCES ORANGE COUNTY DISTILLERY WHEAT VODKA

1 OUNCE TRIPLE-PEPPERED SYRUP (PAGE 99)

2 DROPS ORANGE FLOWER WATER

1 EGG WHITE

3 PINCHES GROUND PEPPER MIX (SEE NOTE)

2 DROPS ANGOSTURA BITTERS

LEMON PEEL

Combine vodka, triple-peppered syrup, orange flower water, and egg white in a cocktail shaker. Dry shake (without ice) for 15 to 20 seconds. Add ice and shake again until chilled. Double-strain into a chilled coupe glass.

Make a "cat face" on the surface of the drink by lightly sprinkling the ground pepper mix to draw the cat's eyes and nose. Add a drop of bitters on either side of the "nose," then carefully drag a cocktail straw or toothpick through the bitters to create the cat's whiskers. Garnish with the lemon peel.

NOTE: To make the ground pepper mix, combine 2 teaspoons black pepper, 1 teaspoon white pepper, and 1 pinch ground red pepper and grind together in a mortar and pestle or spice grinder.

FROM ORANGE COUNTY DISTILLERY AT
BROWN BARN FARMS | NEW HAMPTON, NEW YORK

CREATED BY NICK SPIEGEL

MAKES 1 DRINK

"YOU TAKE OVER
MY HOUSE AND HOME
YOU EVEN TRY TO ANSWER
MY TELEPHONE
DELILAH, YOU'RE THE
APPLE OF MY EYES"

—QUEEN, "DELILAH"

PIZZA

PIZZA PATCHES

CORSAIR DISTILLERY | NASHVILLE, TENNESSEE

Darek Bell, owner and distiller of Corsair Distillery, had talked about bringing in a distillery cat to help with rodent control when a distinctive looking tortoiseshell cat started hanging around the building. She introduced herself by sneaking in and stealing food, including scraps of meatballs, prosciutto, macaroni, and, as fate would have it, pizza.

"She is a badass. She strolled in and decided this was the place for her. We had little say in the matter. She showed up one day and never left. It was a hostile takeover on her part." One of the distillers thought her colorful coat looked like a pizza loaded with extra toppings, and the name stuck.

Pizza, who has become of a bit of a dandy with her trademark kerchief or bespoke bow tie, maintains a busy schedule of sleeping on barrels, grain sacks, and the occasional human lap (but only if you've earned her respect). She always rouses herself to stop by during distillery tours, but primarily it's for comic relief, upstaging the person giving the tour to ensure she remains the center of attention.

While she's proven to be a "weapon of mass rodent destruction," Pizza's even better at stealing sandwiches from the employee break room (especially from unsuspecting new hires and interns). Making off with so many snacks has had its toll. "She has gotten a little chubby lately," admits Bell. "She was climbing around the ceiling titles and broke through, falling onto a stunned guest at the bar. Luckily nobody was hurt, and the guest, a regular, thought it was funny."

"TO BE CLEAR, THIS IS *MY* DISTILLERY. I JUST LET YOU HANG OUT HERE."

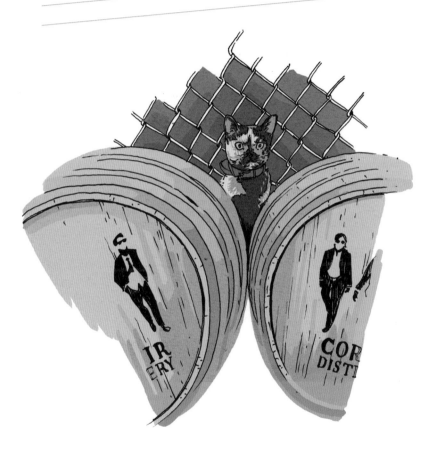

5 YEARS OLD

TORTOISESHELL

FEMALE

CATEGORY DISTILLERY CAT

JOB TITLE HEAD MOUSER

FAVORITE SNACK PIZZA (NATCH)

FAVORITE TOY HUMAN BEINGS (THEY'RE SO EASY TO MANIPULATE)

SUPERPOWER MAJOR "TORTITUDE"

GIN'S GOTTA NICE PEAR

1½ OUNCES PEAR-INFUSED CORSAIR GIN
(SEE NOTE)

¾ OUNCE FRESH LEMON JUICE

½ OUNCE HONEY

FRESH ROSEMARY SPRIG

Combine the gin, lemon juice, and honey in a cocktail shaker filled with ice. Shake until chilled and then strain into a chilled coupe glass. Garnish with the rosemary sprig.

NOTE: To make the pear-infused gin, add one pear (cut into large chunks) to the bottom of a large glass bottle or jar with a lid. Cover with one bottle of gin (reserving the bottle) and allow to infuse for 72 hours. Add a cinnamon stick and a fresh sprig of rosemary and infuse for another 24 hours. Strain the pear-infused gin back into the original bottle, discarding the solids.

FROM CORSAIR DISTILLERY | NASHVILLE, TENNESSEE

MAKES 1 DRINK

"NASHVILLE CATS,
PLAY CLEAN AS
COUNTRY WATER
NASHVILLE CATS,
PLAY WILD AS
MOUNTAIN DEW"

—THE LOVIN' SPOONFUL, "NASHVILLE CATS"

"MOST FOLKS THAT DON'T LIKE CATS LIKE THE SCRATCH."

9 YEARS OLD

TUXEDO

FEMALE

CATEGORY DISTILLERY CAT

JOB TITLE TOO MANY TO LIST

FAVORITE TOY COCKTAIL STRAWS

HOBBY SUNBEAMS

I'M REALLY INTO . . . LAP-BASED BACK RUBS

SUPERPOWER CUSTOMER RELATIONS

SCRATCHY
THE SCRATCH

INDUSTRY CITY DISTILLERY | BROOKLYN, NEW YORK
ARCANE DISTILLING | BROOKLYN, NEW YORK

Scratchy does double-duty as distillery cat at two businesses that share the same space: Industry City Distillery and Arcane Distilling. As David Kyrejko, who works at both venues (engineer at ICD, distiller at Arcane) and spends a lot of time with "the Scratch" will tell you, "two distilleries sharing 12,000 square feet makes for lots of hiding spots."

Scratchy began her life as the "esteemed mouser" at the Spotted Pig in the West Village. Chef April Bloomfield dubbed her Scratchins Black (a nod to the British slang for table scraps), but everyone knows her as Scratchy. When Scratchy's previous owner, restaurateur Ken Friedman, could no longer keep the cat and put it out there that she needed a home, Kyrejko was sold. "I wanted a social cat that wasn't too 'mushy.' Scratch has some lap-cat tendencies but also has the feisty hunter streak. Given her vast experience in food service, I thought she'd fit in just fine."

As the two distilleries share a floor in the same building, Scratchy tends to wear a lot of different hats in the operation, from head distiller to chief marketing officer to shop foreman to lab cat. "She's basically the entire marketing department for Industry City Distillery and is my late-night lab helper over at Arcane." On weekends, she's devoted to full-time customer relations, when, as the de facto face of Industry City Distillery, her primary job is to hang around the tasting room to greet visitors. "Scratchy is unusually social. She comes when called and actually loves crowds. She spends most of her time lounging on one of the tasting room tables and will also just sort of hang with patrons. They love it. It's amazing what having a cat can do when someone is waiting in line for a cocktail."

SUGAR MAPLE
SHUGGIE

NELSON'S GREEN BRIER DISTILLERY | NASHVILLE, TENNESSEE

Nelson's Green Brier Distillery makes Tennessee whiskey filtered through sugar maple charcoal, so Sugar Maple seemed like the perfect name for a distillery cat. The Maine coon mix who has that name was a street cat who wound up at the Nashville Humane Association before being adopted by head distiller Andy Nelson a couple of months after the distillery's grand opening. "Rescue cats have an excellent track record of being hard-nosed enforcers who give rodents no quarter." And did she live up to expectations? "There were a few mice and rats running around before we got her, but she has absolutely curbed that activity. We have yet to find a mouse in a trap since she's been on the prowl."

The first person to enter the distillery each morning gets a special greeting from Sugar Maple, but Nelson is quick to point out, "It's usually not out of true love; mostly just out of hunger." After at least a dozen naps and several stretching sessions, she'll sprint around the office for exercise but saves most of her energy for the after-hours night patrol when she has the barrel warehouse and production floor to herself. "We tried letting her out during the daytime when guests are taking tours, but she stole the attention away from the tour guides. She tends to climb up on pallets and pose for photos, which is great and all, but it's a bit distracting."

"I'D RATHER BE NAPPING."

3½ YEARS OLD

MAINE COON

FEMALE

CATEGORY DISTILLERY CAT

JOB TITLE NIGHTSHIFT MANAGER

FAVORITE TOY ANY LIVE RODENT

HOBBY CARDBOARD BOXES

I'M REALLY INTO . . . THE SINK

CATERWAUL

1½ OUNCES BELLE MEADE BOURBON

¾ OUNCE ZUCCA

¾ OUNCE COCCHI VERMOUTH DI TORINO

¾ OUNCE ROTHMAN & WINTER
ORCHARD APRICOT LIQUEUR

LEMON PEEL

Combine all of the ingredients except the lemon peel in a
mixing glass filled with ice. Stir until chilled and then strain
into a chilled coupe glass. Garnish with the lemon peel.

FROM NELSON'S GREEN BRIER DISTILLERY
NASHVILLE, TENNESSEE
MAKES 1 DRINK

"KRAZY KAT PEEKING
THROUGH A LACE BANDANA
LIKE A ONE-EYED
CHESHIRE
LIKE A DIAMOND-EYED
JACK"

—THE GRATEFUL DEAD, "CHINA CAT SUNFLOWER"

"WHO YOU GONNA CALL?"

2½ YEARS OLD

TABBY

MALE

CATEGORY BREWERY CAT

JOB TITLE HEAD BREWERY CAT

FAVORITE TOY TOWEL SPRINKLED WITH CATNIP

HOBBY CARDBOARD

SUPERPOWER MAKES RATS DISAPPEAR

VENKMAN

Like many brewers and distillers housing hundred-pound bags of expensive grain, Bill Hurley, CEO of Empirical Brewery, had a rat problem. "We were sick of living with giant rats. When the exterminator was successful, we had dead rats in our building. When they weren't, we had chewed-up grain bags we had to throw out." After exploring professional extermination solutions, he eventually contacted the Tree House Humane Society, whose Cats at Work program pairs captured feral cats with businesses seeking a more unconventional (though organic) way to keep their intruding rodent population in check.

Empirical was matched with a quartet of feral cats (three boys and a girl). The felines began a systematic process of acclimation into their new home before they were turned loose in the distillery. When Empirical took to social media for feedback on what to name the new tenants, the Ghostbusters Cats (Venkman, Ray, Egon, and Gozer) won out over other categories like Cartoon Villains, Famous Astronomers, and Beer Scientists. As feral cats, they're not socialized for human interaction, but they roam around the distillery after dark, and Hurley constructed a handmade, multitiered cat condo (with plenty of safe hiding places), dubbed the Dark Tower, for them to enjoy.

Sadly, Gozer, the littlest cat, passed away, leaving behind Venkman and his two brothers. While they're all adorable, Hurley sums up the cats' personalities this way: "Venkman likes to be left alone. Ray likes to be petted. Egon doesn't even like to be looked at." While still skittish by most distillery cat standards, Venkman has stepped into his role as head brewery cat. He even has his own Twitter account (@VenkmanTheCat) and has become of a bit of a reluctant celebrity, featured on CNN and the *Wall Street Journal* as a shining example of successfully transitioning feral cats into the workplace.

VERBAL
KITTY SÖZE

TENTH WARD DISTILLING COMPANY | FREDERICK, MARYLAND

After being unceremoniously abandoned by his first family, who left him behind with nothing but a bag of cat food thrown on the neighbor's porch when they moved, Verbal was rescued by Monica Pearce and Kyle Pfalzer on the opening weekend of their distillery, Tenth Ward Distilling Company. He managed to fit right in, catching a mouse within his first week of employment. While he likes to talk a lot, his name is primarily a nod to Kevin Spacey's unassuming conman character in *The Usual Suspects*, Roger "Verbal" Kint, whose mysterious, murderous alter ego (spoiler alert!) turns out to be the infamous gangland bogeyman, Keyser Söze. The name seems especially fitting when you review Verbal's "Kitty Söze Death Toll," written out in hash marks on an office dry-erase board: "Mice (14), Cicadas (7), Grasshoppers (6), Moths (1), Beetles (3), Dunno (1)."

Verbal lives in the distillery, though he spends much of the day wandering the block, visiting neighboring businesses. But at the distillery, he takes full advantage of the barrel racks to climb around and the many grain bags to nap on. The first week on the job, he went missing and, just as Kyle and Monica were preparing to call local shelters, his little head peeked over the edge of an empty grain bag directly behind Kyle. Since then, he's become a definitive people person, following everyone around like a dog. He'll even hop into the car and accompany the team on whiskey deliveries.

But Verbal knows how to make an entrance like only a cat can, like the time he came through the kitty door with a live baby mouse between his teeth and deposited it in front of a visiting tour group. Grabbing a broom, Kyle quickly shuffled both Verbal and the dazed mouse out the back door.

Kitty soze Death Toll

Mice: |||| |||| ||||
Cicadas: |||| ||
Grasshoppers: |||| |
Moths: |
Dunno: |
Beetle: |||

4 YEARS OLD

GRAY & WHITE

MALE

CATEGORY DISTILLERY CAT

FAVORITE PLACE TO BE SCRATCHED ON THE CHIN

FAVORITE TOY FEATHERS ON A STRING ATTACHED TO A REMOTE-CONTROLLED CAR

NOTABLE FEATURE SNAGGLETOOTH

TAKES HIS WHISKEY . . . IN A SAUCER

SUPERPOWER MAKING AN ENTRANCE

BLOODY MANHATTAN

2 OUNCES TENTH WARD DISTILLING COMPANY
WHITE CARAWAY RYE

¾ OUNCE SOLERNO BLOOD ORANGE LIQUEUR

¼ OUNCE SWEET VERMOUTH

1 DASH ORANGE BITTERS

ORANGE SLICE (BLOOD ORANGE IF IN SEASON)

Combine all of the ingredients except the orange slice in a
mixing glass filled with ice. Stir until chilled and then strain
into a chilled coupe glass. Garnish with the orange slice.

FROM TENTH WARD DISTILLING COMPANY
FREDERICK, MARYLAND

MAKES 1 DRINK

"*MEOW* MEANS *WOOF* IN CAT."

—GEORGE CARLIN

SYRUPS

GINGER SYRUP

1 CUP GRANULATED SUGAR
1 CUP WATER
2 (3-INCH) KNOBS OF GINGER, PEELED AND SLICED INTO COINS

Combine the sugar, water, and ginger in a medium saucepan and
bring to a simmer, stirring occasionally to dissolve the sugar.
At the first crack of a boil, remove from the heat. Let cool
completely, pour through a strainer into a glass jar with a lid.
The syrup will keep in the refrigerator for up to 1 month.

MAKES 1½ CUPS

DEMERARA SYRUP

2 CUPS DEMERARA SUGAR
1 CUP WATER

Combine the sugar and water in a medium saucepan and bring
to a simmer, stirring occasionally to dissolve the sugar.
At the first crack of a boil, remove from the heat. Let cool
completely, then pour into a glass jar with a lid. The syrup
will keep in the refrigerator for up to 1 month.

MAKES 1½ CUPS

SIMPLE SYRUP

1 CUP GRANULATED SUGAR
1 CUP WATER

Combine the sugar and water in a medium saucepan and bring
to a simmer, stirring occasionally to dissolve the sugar. At the first
crack of a boil, remove from the heat. Let cool completely,
then pour into a glass jar with a lid. The syrup will keep
in the refrigerator for up to 1 month.

MAKES 1½ CUPS

TRIPLE-PEPPERED SYRUP

1½ CUPS GRANULATED SUGAR
1 CUP WATER
2 TEASPOONS FRESHLY GROUND BLACK PEPPER
1 TEASPOON FRESHLY GROUND WHITE PEPPER
1 PINCH GROUND RED PEPPER

Combine all the ingredients in a medium saucepan and bring to a
simmer, stirring occasionally to dissolve the sugar. At the first crack
of a boil, remove from the heat. Let cool completely, then pour
through a strainer into a glass jar with a lid; discard the solids. The
syrup will keep refrigerated for up to 1 month.

MAKES APPROXIMATELY 2 CUPS

FEATURED DISTILLERIES & BREWERIES

2SP BREWING COMPANY
120 Concord Road, Units 101–103
Aston, PA 19014
(484) 483-7860
www.2spbrewing.com
@2spbrewing
Cat: Brewery Cat
@BreweryCat2SP

ALBANY DISTILLING CO.
78 Montgomery Street
Albany, NY 12207
(518) 621-7191
www.albanydistilling.com
@AlbanyDistillingCo
Cat: Cooper

ARCANE DISTILLING
33 35th Street
Brooklyn, NY 11232
(718) 490-6171
www.arcanedistilling.com
@Arcane_NYC
Cat: Scratchy | @TheScratchy

CORSAIR DISTILLERY
601 Merritt Avenue
Nashville, TN 37203
(615) 200-0320
www.corsairdistillery.com
@CorsairDistillery
Cat: Copper
1200 Clinton Street
Nashville, TN 37203
Cat: Pizza

CREATURE COMFORTS BREWING CO.
271 West Hancock Avenue
Athens, GA 30601
(706) 410-1043
www.creaturecomfortsbeer.com
@creaturecomfortsbeer
Cat: Automatic
@AutoTheBreweryCat

DUCLAW BREWING CO.
8901 Yellow Brick Road, Suite B
Baltimore, MD 21237
(443) 559-9900
www.duclaw.com
@duclawbrewingco
Cats: The DuClaws (Mosaic,
Simcoe, HellRazer & Bock)
@Hellrazer_and_the_Duclaws

EMPIRICAL BREWERY
1801 West Foster Avenue
Chicago, IL 60640
(773) 654-3104
www.empiricalbrewery.com
@empiricalbrew
Cat: Venkman | @VenkmanTheCat

**THE GUARDIAN BREWING
COMPANY**
2100 West White River Boulevard
Muncie, IN 47303
(765) 896-8235
www.theguardianbrewingco.com
@the_guardian_brewing_co
Cat: Brewster
@BrewsterTheBrewCat

HAMILTON DISTILLERS
2106 Forbes Boulevard, #103
Tucson, AZ 85745
(520) 628-9244
www.hamiltondistillers.com
@HamiltonDistillers
Cats: Masher and Two-Row

**HOTEL TANGO ARTISAN
DISTILLERY**
702 Virginia Avenue
Indianapolis, IN 46203
(317) 653-1806
www.hoteltangowhiskey.com
@HotelTangoIndy
Cat: Fletcher Pickles
@HotelTangoCat

INDUSTRY CITY DISTILLERY
33 35th Street, #6A
Brooklyn, NY 11232
(718) 305-6951
www.industrycitydistillery.com
@DrinkICD
Cat: Scratchy | @TheScratchy

KINGS COUNTY DISTILLERY
299 Sands Street, Building 121
Brooklyn, NY 11205
(347) 689-4211
www.kingscountydistillery.com
@KingsCountyDistillery
Cat: Jeffy

LUCKY HARE BREWING COMPANY
6085 Beckhorn Road
Hector, NY 14841
(610) 613-8424
www.luckyharebrewing.com
@LuckyHareBrewing
Cat: Daryl Hall

MIDDLE WEST SPIRITS
1230 Courtland Avenue
Columbus, OH 43201
(614) 299-2460
www.middlewestspirits.com
@MiddleWestSpirits
Cats: Hancock and Hemingway

**NELSON'S GREEN BRIER
DISTILLERY**
1414 Clinton Street
Nashville, TN 37203
(615) 913-8800
www.greenbrierdistillery.com
@TNWhiskeyCo
Cat: Sugar Maple
@SugarMapleCat

NEVERSINK SPIRITS
33 New Broad Street
Port Chester, NY 10573
(914) 352-1953
www.neversinkspirits.com
@NeversinkSpirits
Cat: General Patton

**NEWBURGH BREWING
COMPANY**
88 South Colden Street
Newburgh, NY 12550
(845) 569-2337
www.newburghbrewing.com
@NewburghBrewing
Cat: Hoodie

**OLDE YORK FARM DISTILLERY
AND COOPERAGE**
284 State Route 23
Hudson, NY 12513
(845) 480-1237
@OldeYorkFarm
Cat: Cork

**ORANGE COUNTY
DISTILLERY**
19B Maloney Lane
Goshen, NY 10924
(845) 651-2929
www.orangecountydistillery.com
@OrangeCountyDistillery
Cat: Pepper

**ORANGE COUNTY DISTILLERY AT
BROWN BARN FARMS**
286 Maple Avenue
New Hampton, NY 10958
(845) 374-2011

OREGON SPIRIT DISTILLERS
740 NE 1st Street
Bend, OR 97701
(541) 382-0002
www.oregonspiritdistillers.com
@OregonSpiritDistillers
Cat: Char

OTHER HALF BREWING CO.
195 Centre Street
Brooklyn, NY 11231
(347) 987-3527
www.otherhalfbrewing.com
@OtherHalfNYC
Cat: Gangsta Cat

ROCKAWAY BREWING COMPANY
46-01 5th Street
Long Island City, NY 11101
(718) 482-6528
www.rockawaybrewco.com
@RockawayBrewCo
Cat: Leland Murphy (RIP)

RUSHING DUCK BREWING CO.
1 Battiato Lane
Chester, NY 10918
(845) 610-5440
www.rushingduck.com
@RushingDuck
Cat: James
@JamesTheBreweryCat

SEATTLE DISTILLING
19429 Vashon Highway SW
Vashon, WA 98070
(206) 463-0830
www.seattledistilling.com
@SeattleDistills
Cat: Castor

SERVICE BREWING CO.
574 Indian Street
Savannah, GA 31401
(912) 358-1002
www.servicebrewing.com
@ServiceBrewing
Cats: Black Hawk and Chinook

SEVENTH SON BREWING CO.
1101 North 4th Street
Columbus, OH 43201
(614) 421-2337
www.seventhsonbrewing.com
@Seventh_Son_Brewing
Cat: Old Horatio
@AssistantManagerCat

SOUND SPIRITS
1138 West Ewing Street, Suite B
Seattle, WA 98119
(206) 651-5166
www.drinksoundspirits.com
@Sound_Spirits
Cat: Cho

TENTH WARD DISTILLING COMPANY
508 East Church Street
Frederick, MD 21701
(301) 662-4297
www.tenthwarddistilling.com
@TenthWardCo
Cat: Verbal

THOMAS & SONS DISTILLERY
4211 SE Milwaukie Avenue
Portland, OR 97202
(503) 477-6137
www.thomasandsonsdistillery.com
@ThomasAndSonsDistillery
Cat: Boone

ZAFTIG BREWING CO.
7020-A Huntley Road
Worthington, OH 43229
(614) 636-2537
www.drinkzaftig.com
@ZaftigBeer
Cat: Hops | @ZaftigHops

ACKNOWLEDGMENTS

Much love to my editor, the super-talented and ever-patient Emily Timberlake. To my publisher, Aaron Wehner, and the team at Ten Speed Press. Thank you, Lizzie Allen, Elisabeth Beller, Windy Dorresteyn, Emma Campion, Allison Renzulli, and Erin Welke.

Thank you to illustrator Julia Kuo for capturing these spirited cats in action and bringing them to life on the page.

A big hug and kiss to my agent, David Black, who always has my back.

To Talia Baiocchi for encouraging me write about the topic in "The Secret Lives of Distillery Cats" on *Punch*.

To Ari Shapiro and Rich Preston for shining the spotlight on the subject in their report, "Behind Every Good Whisky Is a Trusty Distillery Cat," on NPR's *All Things Considered*. (RIP Peat.)

Thanks to all the distillery cats and brewery cats who agreed to be interviewed for this project, and to their human caretakers who helped facilitate with stories, photographs, and cocktail recipes. And to everyone who follows my continued chronicles of all the working-cat action @DistilleryCats.

Finally, to the beloved cats of my past, Waldo and Wushu, who were there for me from boyhood through adulthood. And to my good friend and roommate, Louis, for being the best cat a guy could ask for, and easily the most handsome.